Early Fatherhood Development

Early Fatherhood Development

by Jeff Yoder

Hysteria Publications
Bridgeport, CT

To my two wonderful children, Kayla and Jacob, without whom I likely would be reduced to writing a humorous book about some wholly undeserving subject like cats or politicians.

Hysteria Publications
P.O. Box 38581
Bridgeport, CT 06605

Tel: (203) 333-9399
Fax: (203) 367-7188
Email: laugh@hysteriabooks.com
Web: http://www.hysteriabooks.com

© 1998 by Jeff Yoder and Hysteria Publications
All rights reserved.
No part of this book may be reproduced
without express written permission from the publisher.

Printed in the United States of America.

ISBN 1-887166-29-7

Cover design by Tom Greensfelder
Cover illustration by Mike Werner
Back cover photograph by Jennifer Harlan
Layout by Brian Best
Proofreading by Nancy Moore Brochin

Contents

"It's a ... Father!" 1
The Hospital 7
The Baby 19
The New You 29
The Courage to Change—Diapers, That Is 35
The Zen of Stuff 41
Got the Time? 49
To Sleep or Not to Sleep 55
Food, Glorious Food 61
Sex (Really!) 67
Family Finances 71
Power, Love, Truth, and All That 75
Mothers-in-Law 81
FAQs—Frequently Asked Questions about Fatherhood 83

Preface

I became a father in 1991 when my daughter, the remarkable Kayla Rose, was born. It has been quite a growth experience. I've learned a lot about what it means to be the one in charge, to have the responsibility of giving direction and advice, sharing wisdom, and running the show. Yes, Kayla is really good at all that.

Three years later my wife gave birth to Batman, but since the name was trademarked we decided to avoid legal entanglements by officially naming him Jacob William. At this writing, Jacob is four years old, which puts his karate chop just about at groin level. (You do not want to be a "bad guy" in our house, unless you are safely in the full fetal position.)

Fatherhood is more than wonderful, but let me tell you, in case no one has clued you in, it's also total lifestyle shock. It drastically changes everything. Goodbye, romantic dining. Goodbye, movies. Goodbye, travel. Goodbye, sleep. They all will be back some day, to be sure, but they will all involve Disney characters in one way or another. Once you can accept that, you can begin to have a sense of humor about it all. I wrote this book for the new father who could use a laugh or at least would like to know he's not the only one whose life has become totally surreal.

It's a wonderful thing, what happens to men when they become fathers. I think it takes us down a peg. We develop over the years this image of who we think we are, or ought to be. Take me, for example. Before I became a father I was, as I think most would have to agree, your basic combination of rock star, super athlete, and romantic stud—and then, more or less overnight, I became the sort of person who goes to work with baby burpings on his shoulder who cannot participate in any conversation whatsoever without interjecting an anecdote about poopy diapers.

I've never been what you would call overly fastidious about my appearance, but I never went into the office with dinosaur stickers on my pants, either. I now consider this perfectly normal attire.

So you have to rethink who you are. You go back to your own childhood and think about what your father was like. But that doesn't really work, because the fathering methods of those times have been largely outlawed. Most forms of routine discipline from those days have been ruled by the Supreme Court to be cruel and unusual punishment—remember spanking? No wonder you turned out to be such a deviant.

Yes, we are now reengineering fatherhood. We're downsizing families, acquiring new roles, merging childcare operations into daycare centers, and generally doing more with less so that we can be more productive.

Anyway, if you're a new father, welcome to the club (of course now we allow women, too). If you're a father-to-be, sleep now. If you're my father, I was just kidding about the spanking stuff.

Jeff Yoder
March 1, 1998

Acknowledgments

My eternal thanks to my kind and gentle yet persistent editor, Lysbeth Guillorn, who gave me deadlines—without which I would still be staring at my bellybutton and contemplating this book—and who had the good sense to cut out the parts that, believe me, you would not have wanted to read. Thanks also to my wife and publisher, who, as fate would have it, are the same person, Deborah Werksman. She helped give birth to this book not only by being the mother of my children but also by encouraging me and, best of all, laughing while she read the manuscript. Now about my advance ...

CHAPTER 1

"It's a ... Father!"

Okay, so what new life form appears at a birth? If you answered "baby," I guess I'm already going a little fast for you. Let's back it up a bit, read the chapter title again. Okay, everyone with us now? So on that magical day of birth you take on a new identity; you're not you anymore, you're a father. Already in the hospital they start referring to you as "the father," like you don't have a name. But more on that later.

This could all be rather daunting if it happened overnight, but not to worry. Fortunately you don't just jump into being a father, there is a training program for it, known as "pregnancy."

The Fatherhood Preparatory Course: Pregnancy

The pregnancy program, designed to prepare you for fatherhood, goes something like this. As we all know, the human gestation period is approximately nine months, which is pretty impressive when you consider it takes even Microsoft about 300 person-years just to make a software program. As at many colleges, this educational program is conveniently divided into trimesters.

The first trimester. This part of the training prepares you for a new being coming into your life, because in the first trimester your wife's body is taken over by an alien. The alien has learned to mimic much of your wife's old behavior, but it cannot conceal its own bizarreness. For one thing, this is when the cravings start. The alien, unlike your health-conscious wife, likes potato chips. You buy potato chips. However, you didn't buy enough potato chips. You need to buy more potato chips.

You buy more. This makes the alien happy. You are beginning to understand that it's important to keep the alien happy. You call the potato chip wholesaler and ask for a truckload of potato chips. You wait tensely for the delivery. The alien is down to its last bag. You run out and buy a few more bags, and as you return, the potato chip truck is pulling into the driveway. You are saved! The alien will be happy right up until childbirth!

But the alien is not happy. Not this alien. The last alien liked potato chips. Now there is a new alien who does not like potato chips. The very thought of potato chips—Ohhh! The grease! The salt! The crunch!—makes the new alien lose its appetite, makes the new alien angry at those who would put such nauseating fare in its face.

What does the new alien want to eat? Please, don't talk about eating. This upsets the alien's stomach. In fact, don't eat. In fact, move the refrigerator out of the house. The presence of food upsets the alien's stomach. This is truly unfortunate, because your wife's midwives would like her to eat 100 grams of protein each day. To eat this much protein, she would have to eat several large animals each day, or enough eggs to feed southern California for Sunday brunch. The midwives do not live with the alien.

The second trimester. Pregnancy? What pregnancy? Okay, this is cool, attend a few childbirth classes, get to play junior obstetrician, contemplate the meaning of life. Cool.

The third trimester. This is really what you think of when you think of pregnancy. What you have here is a large, uncomfortable woman who cannot move without third-party assistance, yet needs to pee every thirteen minutes because someone is sitting on her bladder, cannot breathe because her lungs have been pushed up into her neck, and is being pummeled from the inside, usually while trying to get to sleep.

If you went to college, you might notice some similarity to the third trimester of your senior year, when panic begins to set in, due to the impending onset of that for which we are seldom adequately prepared—reality.

One day, someone gives you a baby present. For me it was a pair of socks. Really small socks. Tiny. And suddenly it dawned on me. I was given these socks to put on feet. Not *my* feet. Feet that are coming, soon. I apologize for making fun of those of you who were slow to pick up on the chapter title. It took me eight and a half months of pregnancy training to get the fact that we were going to have, in our actual house, an actual human baby.

Meanwhile, as you're absorbing the reality shock, your wife is going from a petite to a size so large it requires its own special type of store. Your house is filling up with things that come from stores and parts of the stores that you never set foot in before. Catalogs are arriving—how did they know?—filled with baby clothes, baby furniture, baby safety devices. What *is* all this stuff?

Many men experience physical symptoms such as nausea that are thought to be sympathetic responses to their wives' pain. I think it's just fear.

Labor Management

You've probably heard all sorts of horror stories about labor. I'm here to tell you that, if you have a choice, you definitely want to be the man during labor. For the man, labor is not really that bad. I mean it just isn't. Let's be honest, nothing happens to *you*. Not physically, anyway. However, I do not recommend that you vocalize this at any time during labor or until well after menopause.

You'll do a lot better, relationship-wise, to focus on the emotional pain you are feeling in sympathy with your wife's suffering. You *do* feel her pain, right? If you don't have any emotions, get some in time for labor.

Medical science has recognized the man's need to feel useful during labor and so has invented a task called "timing the contractions." This makes childbirth one of the few major life events for which it is considered in good taste to use a stopwatch.

Yes, labor is a very good time to be a man, except for one thing. Your wife knows that she is the only one in pain, and you know it too. This does not fit in with our protective instincts. We guys are supposed to protect our wives from life's little discomforts, and certain parties who are in the throes of tidal waves of raw pain may perceive that we have dropped the ball on this one and get just the teensiest bit irritated. For example, I did find that my wife was a bit annoyed, in a shrieking sort of way, about the length of time I was gone when I went out to get some vital birthing supplies of some sort, like film for the camera or something. Not that labor is an emotionally charged time, or anything, but seven years later she still brings this up: "There I was, about to have the baby any second, and where were you?" (Actually, the baby wasn't born until almost the next day, but that's irrelevant.)

I guarantee you one thing: You will not do labor right. There *is* no right way to do it, as far as I can see. Just be there and take it like a man.

Oh, and Birth

So even with the baby toys and the tiny socks and all the stuff that had shown up, even with my wife having doubled in size, even with feeling the kicking, hearing the heartbeat, it was not really real for me that we were having a baby until the top of that little head appeared. And then the whole head. It was a little girl, and she looked just like my father-in-law. I cried, in a restrained, guy-like way. Not because it was a girl, not even because she looked like my father-in-law—but because on some level I was now aware that, suddenly, my life wasn't about me anymore.

Clueing in to the New Fatherhood

If you are a new father, the good news is, you are not alone. The bad news is, most new fathers are just as clueless as you are. And if you think you aren't clueless, that just shows how *really* clueless you are. And if you find that logic circular, go back to the beginning of this sentence and read it again.

Hey, there's no shame in being clueless about fatherhood. After all, it's a brand new concept, invented in the 1990s, which is loosely based on the fatherhood of your father's generation, but now it's actually taken on the verb form, fathering. Believe me, if I named this book something about "Fathering" you'd be browsing through "Great Football Moments of the 1970s" right now. Like you're not busy enough—now you have to *father*? I rather like the term "Fatherhood" myself—it suggests a noble state of being, sort of like Knighthood, rather than an action.

So the new version of fatherhood goes like this. You do all the wonderful things your father did—provide for the family, roll on the floor with the kids, be a role model of moral rectitude (or whatever it was *your* father did)—and, and, and, you now also are responsible for sharing all the tasks your mother did, such as diapering, feeding, burping, cooking, cleaning, shopping, medical care, and psychological counseling.

Yes, now dads are more involved in both domestic affairs and child-rearing, and if you wonder why it's called rearing, see the chapter on diapers.

About the only preparation for fatherhood that might alleviate prenatal male parent cluelessness would be working in a twenty-four-hour day-care facility run by your wife, with part-time staffing from your in-laws, where you work sixteen hour shifts and in your eight hours off, you work another job where you earn money to support the day-care facility.

So, to help other fathers maintain a sense of humor through these life-altering times, I committed to writing down my experiences during my early years of fatherhood.

A little secret that we first-time fathers will never admit is that when we become fathers a lot of us finally get to become what we really wanted to be all along, and it's actually a tremendous relief because we no longer have to prove that we're, you know, what guys try to prove they are. "Sorry, George, I can't go bungee-jumping today ... new baby, you understand." In fact, I almost was going to call this book *Soul Soup for Chickens*. A lot of us try to pretend we're tough guys (pa-*tooooey*), but deep down that new little person is the most important thing in the world to us. The other title I thought of was *What to Expect When You're Expectorating*.

Chapter Quiz: The New Father

Yes, throughout this book there are quizzes. If this causes you to hyperventilate: Remember, you can always cheat. The correct answers are a, b, c, or d, not necessarily in that order.

1. The reason fatherhood is different nowadays is:
   a. Traditional roles have changed to accommodate the two-income family.
   b. Fathers today have learned to be sensitive, nurturing, and intimate.
   c. Your father had better sense than to bungee-jump in the first place.
   d. There are mothers like Madonna.

2. Your role as a new father is:
   a. Be sensitive.
   b. Be nurturing.
   c. Be cool.
   d. Be boppa ree bop.

See? That wasn't so bad. Besides, there *are* no right answers—this isn't like when *you* were a kid!

Chapter 2

The Hospital

Why We Need Hospitals

Unless you're one of those countercultural wacko naturalist-types who think babies can be born at home (like, for example, our grandmothers and all of the women in human history before them), you know that babies must be born in the hospital.

After all, with home birth, you take your chances with the forces of nature. In the hospital, nature is safely controlled, and instead you take your chances with third-year medical students who haven't slept since before your child's conception took place, and who may yet drop out and go to law school so they can make some *real* money.

But it's a lucky thing we have hospitals, or where would we get those funny little skull caps that newborns wear?

Childbirth—A Guy Thing

If you remember the childbirth scene in *Gone with the Wind*, you can picture the old model of birthing, consisting of women with bowls of hot water and clean towels who, with a combination of instinct and handed-down wisdom, competently cared for the birthing mother, even if they didn't know nothin' 'bout birthin' no babies. That was before the invention of healthcare, which for better or worse was pretty much invented by men. Now, if you have taken Radical Feminism 101, you have learned that hospitals are run based on a male medical model in which men have attempted to take control of the ultimate form of female power—childbirth. (For extra credit, try saying "male medical model" three times real fast.) I believe there may be something to the Rad Fem theory, given the large array of metal tools used in the average childbirth.

Also, I have seen films of Brazilian women birthing babies, *all by themselves*. They just sort of squat and the babies pop out. Gravity plays a role here, and so does squatting, which is a fairly instinctive way of getting things out of the lower part of your body.

However, in hospitals, women lie flat on their backs with their legs up in the air (is this a man's idea, or what?) and are expected to push out a baby this way. Of course it's difficult to do in this position, so there's this tool, called a forceps, with which the birthing professional can go in there and grab the baby by the head and yank it out the way you would change an oil filter.

In ancient times, women took care of childbirth and men had the good sense to stay as far away as possible, which led to the invention of golf. Men really are better at putting things into things than getting things out of things.

It wasn't just the doctors who thought hospital birthing was a good idea—fathers did too, once upon a time. The '50s dad had it easy: drive wife to the hospital, hand her over to trained professionals, then sit down and smoke nervously for a few hours, while preparing the legal papers for suing the tobacco company thirty-five years later. When the doctor announces the news, call your secretary to have her buy the appropriate colored ribbons, pink or blue, to tie around the cigars. Nowadays, we don't smoke, and if we do, we don't inhale, and ... we only smoke cigars that are so expensive our fathers would have scoffed at such extravagance.

The new father of today probably knows more about labor and delivery than your mother's obstetrician did, although the obstetrician definitely knew more about sedatives. Today's father has, at a minimum, attended Lamaze classes so he can be prepared to coach his laboring wife on to victory. He may have even seen films of actual childbirth, an event which would have made his father run with fear, if hospitals had allowed a father to even be in the same wing as the delivery room. Try telling your father that you are going to be there during the delivery of your child. I guarantee he will say, "Why would you want to do that? I suggest you stay as far away from there as possible."

But the new father does not fear the feral energy of the birthing woman, the sight of blood, or even the afterbirth (something which your father does not even know about, during which, following the delivery of the baby, the woman gives birth to the placenta, which is basically a disposable liver). The new father wants to be there for his own life, to experience the mystery and wonder of childbirth. And, fortunately, hospitals are still equipped with smelling salts.

Surviving Childbirth–For Dad, That Is

My childbirth suggestions for the new Dad are as follows.

Regarding feral birthing energy: Just make sure there are no blunt instruments in the room with which your wife could hit you, and you'll be fine, providing you can withstand being yelled at by a cross between a marine drill sergeant and Godzilla.

Regarding the sight of blood: If you watch television or go to movies this shouldn't be a problem, although it's a little more personal when it's your wife; for me, watching the birth videos at our prenatal class helped (once I came to), as did the fact that I was a nose-bleeder as a kid.

Regarding the afterbirth: I don't watch the kind of movies that might prepare you for the sight of an internal organ plopping into the room, but fortunately this happens after the birth of the baby, so nothing much will faze you at this point. However, I strongly suggest leaving this one to the birthing professionals. (I will mention in passing that some who are more radical than this new dad actually believe it to be good luck to save the placenta and serve it up with onions and mushrooms. I hereby declare this optional. If you want to save the placenta and plant it in with a new tree, that is a wonderful, symbolic thing to do. We did this with both births. That is, we intend to, as soon as we find a place in our yard to plant a tree. In the meantime, we have two pieces of Tupperware that have been out of circulation for several years, in the freezer, labeled "Human body parts: DO NOT EAT.")

Surviving Medical Technology

One of the problems with medical technology is that it has eclipsed certain skills that care givers used to have. We had the revealing experience of going through the entire series of prenatal visits with both an obstetrician and, separately, a team of lay midwives. Lay midwives are women with no medical training whatsoever, other than having studied the subject of childbirth with utter devotion their entire lives, read every book on the subject in the world, apprenticed for many years, and probably birthed hundreds or even thousands of babies.

Our highly trained obstetrician, meanwhile, was unable to detect the heartbeat of our baby for many weeks after the lay midwives had not only found it but let us hear it, too. The obstetrician constantly urged us to do a sonogram so she could tell the position of the baby, while our midwives could figure it out by using their hands. Of course, this may have had something to do with the fact that the obstetrician spent about four nanoseconds with us on each visit, while the team of three midwives all spent an hour with us each time. I kept wondering, don't they have real jobs? How can they make money doing this? You'd think they got some kind of kick out of helping people.

The thing to remember about hospitals is that, while *you* (naively) may think of childbirth as a natural or even spiritual event, the hospital considers it to be a medical emergency, on the order of an appendectomy. Hospitals are good at fixing you when you're broken but not too good about helping you when you're perfectly healthy. Just take a look at the meals they serve and you'll see what I mean.

You may want to seriously consider finding a good team of midwives and having your birth at home like your grandmother did. However, if you do find yourself in the hospital, be sure to be armed with:

The Birthing Plan

The well-informed birthing consumers these days do not just go into the hospital and throw themselves on the mercy of the medical profession. No, we go in with a Birthing Plan that we expect the hospital, as public servant, to execute. You develop a Birthing Plan after you have totally educated yourself about the birthing process, to ensure that you will have the ideal birth experience. It's kind of like a business plan. Actually, it's kind of like developing a business plan while you are in an MBA program and then going out into the real world and executing it while you are strapped to the front of a speeding locomotive headed directly for a tractor trailer that is stalled on the tracks. And as the train is speeding toward certain destruction, your wife has become a raving lunatic and there is no sane person in sight for miles except you, and you're a few doughnuts short of a dozen yourself at the moment. The Birthing Plan is intended to help you remember under these circumstances the ideal birth you had envisioned.

Our Birthing Plan for our first child was designed to create the totally natural childbirth experience: no drugs, no fetal monitoring, baby stays with mother, nursing on demand, sanskrit chanting in the background, that sort of thing. Basically we wanted no medical intervention whatsoever, and in fact we had planned on a home birth but my wife went into a sort of permanent labor state which lasted for what seemed to be about a month, with no apparent end in sight and it truly seemed like the baby would just never arrive without the use of explosives, like the baby had decided to just set up shop on the inside and become the world's first human to remain unborn for its entire life, or maybe until it was a teenager, at which point out it would arrive, complete with tattoos and pierced navel, or pierced umbilical cord, and head straight for the mall.

So we went to the hospital and let them blast away. But we stuck to our game plan to make Vince Lombardi proud. The hospital staff looked at us like, so what did you come to the hospital *for*, anyway?

The part of the Plan that has to do with dealing with the hospital is not so bad, if you keep your wits about you, which of course you won't. The really tricky part is when your wife is screaming "Give me drugs! Give me drugs!" and you have to say, "Remember dear, earlier on you thought it would be best if … I mean we both agreed that … you told me that no matter what you said during the birth you wanted me to make sure that … aaarrrgggghhhhhhh! Your teeth! My thigh! Biting was not in the Plan!"

So, okay, most of us parents-to-be end up in the maternity ward and one way or another the baby comes out. That being the case, let me point out a few things you definitely want to watch out for in the hospital.

The Joy of C-sections

Cesarean sections sort of take the pain of vaginal delivery and spread it out over three or four months, not counting any psychological implications. If this was Julius Caesar's idea, I can see why Brutus tried to perform one on him, even though he wasn't pregnant at the time.

While I suspect that many C-sections are the result of the hospital legal staff being more skilled than the medical staff, I must in all honesty admit that there do seem to be cases where they are better than the alternative, which is to leave things to Ma Nature. The problem here is that Ma Nature is not exactly a mother in the idealized human sense. She has a tendency to always be looking at the bigger picture, sort of from a systems perspective, and is not overly concerned with the well-being of any one particular mortal at any particular time, which is somewhat disconcerting when the mortal in question files a joint tax return with you.

Jacob, like his sister, was planning to be born sometime around sixteen years of gestation, and while we had managed to get Kayla to make her grand entrance actually through the birth canal, Jake was facing the wrong way and also seemed to leave his elbows up, or maybe crossed in defiance, thereby rendering him a lot wider than the exit could accommodate. My wife is now planning an extensive tattoo to decorate her scar, and my son was born without a pointy head.

Breastfeeding "Advice" Pamphlets

Always consider the source when reading any kind of informative literature. Ironically, the breastfeeding "advice" pamphlets that are carefully left for the new mother to discover in her hospital room are published by the very same people who would be out of business if everyone actually did breastfeed—that's right, the formula companies. How nice of them! Yes, they seem to have altruistically overcome the profit motive to be sure you are fully informed about nature's perfect food, and mainly to be sure every mother is aware of what to do about sore nipples, leaking nipples, breast-pumping, mastitis ... and, if for some strange reason she doesn't want to have to deal with all these mammalian horrors, they just happen to have a product for her: the Orwellian-sounding Formula.

If somebody told me I had to drink something called Formula, created by the drug companies, I would request to be beamed up. But then I do have my contrarian streak. I'm still suspicious of vitamins—I mean, you pretty much have to take it on faith that anything has vitamins in it.

However, if you are in fact looking for breastfeeding information, and you are the person in the family with breasts, the place to get it is clearly La Leche League. One cautionary note, though. My wife came back from her first La Leche League meeting in tears. This was while she was still pregnant with Kayla. "Our life is ruined!" she said. "All those children—crying, demanding attention, screaming! Our life is over! What have we done?"

"Relax, dear," I assured her, "we're only having one." I just love being wise.

The problem is, two weeks after Kayla was born, my wife was in tears again. "Our life is ruined! Our life is over! What have we done?"

Okay, this time she had me. Not to worry, though—that was just one of those little dark nights of the soul. It got better. In fact our entire social circle now consists of families we met through La Leche League. What we hadn't been prepared for is that in fact our life as we knew it *was* over, and now we were being dragged kicking and screaming into a new one. This is how the Shiva force works. Shiva is the ancient Hindu god of destruction who is also the god of creation. When something is destroyed, something else is created. When something is created, something else is destroyed. Modern physics says the same thing. The great truths of religion and science at the highest level are one. But you won't necessarily find them in hospital pamphlets.

Hospital "Food"

The apparent fear of breastfeeding in hospitals may seem strange, but actually it begins to make sense once you more fully understand the hospital's overall nutritional program. You might think that hospitals would be the first to serve health food ... whole grains, maybe, with organic fruits and vegetables, that kind of thing. Ha! How naive of you! Hospitals couldn't care less about something as trendy as health. Health is bad for the healthcare business.

Our hospital had a room labeled "Nutrition," which in fact was nothing more than a snack kitchen containing such nutritive substances as Jell-O, soda, coffee, and high-fructose corn syrup "juice" drinks with artificial flavoring and coloring. You could have consumed every item in the entire Nutrition room with absolutely no fear of accidentally ingesting a nutrient. Jell-O, made from boiled pig hide (you think I'm kidding?) is the number one hospital food, and probably the only product containing pig ingredients to be certified Kosher.

Circumcision–A Great Idea or What?

I know you're probably thinking that this topic has nothing to do with this chapter, but wait and see how I bring it right around to make a point about whatever the point of this chapter is.

There is definitely a school of thought that says, hey, we have just produced a perfect little baby, why go making alterations?

There is another school of thought that says, well, they routinely do it in American hospitals, so it *must* be totally necessary, right?

My main problem with schools of thought is that when there is more than one of them, you have to think—that is, if you are *aware* that there is more than one. Now, for most people, I believe, this is not a big problem because most normal people kind of go along with the mainstream, listen to their doctor, and life is relatively decision-free.

Not in my house. If we are planning to, say, get our child a haircut, my wife will go to the library and find thirteen books on haircuts, six of which say haircuts are deadly, four of which say they're potentially dangerous but with proper planning you can improve your odds, and two of which say that you will die an untimely death if you do not have your hair trimmed regularly (these are published by the American Barber and Beauty Association). I know that only adds up to twelve—we still can't find the other book, and it's three years overdue.

So in our family we go to great pains to question everything, especially when it comes to modern medicine. I mean, we even question the germ theory of disease. You probably didn't even know it was just a theory.

Now let me tell you, you read the literature on circumcision and I guarantee your decision-making engine will seize up and you will become the scarecrow in *The Wizard of Oz* ("This way is nice; that way is nice too; although people do go both ways"). One book was titled something like, *Circumcision—Institutionalized Child Mutilation*, another was called *Circumcision—The Greatest Medical Practice Since Sliced Bread (No Pun Intended)*, and another one was *Circumcision—Maybe or Maybe Not, You Decide and Let Your Child Live with the Consequences Forever.*

Thank God my wife is Jewish, so that pretty much settled it in the end, but not after great agonizing. I would say, in general, that when you are faced with 19,000 or so years of tradition versus a burning personal intellectual and moral conviction to question authority and examine your actions, it is definitely way easier to do what everyone else wants you to do.

So we went with Jewish tradition, which has some definite advantages in the circumcision area, namely that our son did not have his foreskin removed in the hospital by just any anonymous medical student, but at home in a ceremonial foreskin removal party, called a *bris*, where the procedure is performed by a special type of rabbi who specializes in ceremonial foreskin removal. This rabbi, called a *moyel*, has probably done more of these than the entire alumni body of Johns Hopkins Medical School.

I must say, the whole thing went pretty smoothly, but then I guess that's easy for me to say.

Chapter Quiz: The Hospital

Here's your chance to test what you have learned in this chapter. In order to boost your self-esteem, assume all your answers are correct.

1. The hospital is designed to:
    a. Make the birthing experience as painless as possible.
    b. Make the birthing experience as expensive as possible.
    c. Introduce a new generation of humans to mistreatment at the hands of the insuro-medical bureaucracy.
    d. Make everyone wish they had beds that tilted up and down.

2. The human race has managed to propagate and grow logarithmically for millions of years because of:
    a. The human sex drive.
    b. Genetic evolution and adaptation to the environment.
    c. Complex hormonal processes in the female of the species designed to ensure proper conception, gestation, and birth.
    d. Hospitals.

3. The best reason to have a home birth is:
    a. To have the baby videotaped emerging into the bosom of his or her extended family.
    b. So you can play esoteric music, light candles, and burn incense in honor of the mystical nature of childbirth.
    c. To be able to advance the laundry between contractions.
    d. Hospitals.

Chapter 3

The Baby

Babies are great. Take my baby ... please! Ha, ha. Just kidding. Babies are beautiful and precious and, with a few simple management techniques, can become productive members of society in just twenty-five or thirty years.

Baby Management

There are two rules pertaining to babies that you must remember at all times. These rules will help you to make strategic decisions at 4 a.m. when you have not slept or eaten for several days and have needed to go to the bathroom since Memorial Day.

Baby Management Rule #1:
Never move a happy baby.

This rule has an important corollary: A *sleeping* baby is a *happy* baby. Therefore, it logically follows that you must never move a sleeping baby. If the baby falls asleep on your lap while you are waiting for a bus or airplane, you must not stand up to board the bus or airplane when it arrives. This will result in certain disaster. This will result in screaming-baby-on-the-bus syndrome or, even worse, screaming-baby-on-the-airplane syndrome or, even worse, your first experience with sky-diving. The correct thing to do is to remain seated until the baby wakes, and catch the next bus or plane, possibly the next day. This will give you plenty of time to come to your senses and just stay close to home.

Baby Management Rule #2:

When the baby is happy, everybody's happy, unless of course you have more than one child.

By the way, I don't mean to imply that babies are happy only when they're sleeping. Babies are inherently happy little beings, *unless* something happens that makes them uncomfortable. These things, and their frequency of occurrence, are presented in the following table:

Source of baby unhappiness	Frequency of occurrence
Hunger	Every forty-five minutes
Stomach gas	After every feeding
Tiredness	Every ninety minutes
Loneliness/boredom	Whenever you walk away
Soiled diaper	Every thirty seconds
And, of course, colic[1]	Whenever you have spent your last reserve of energy and are borderline hysterical with a mild but worsening case of pneumonia, brought on by the stress associated with the fear of losing your job if you don't get some sleep.

From what I'm writing you might assume that I find babies to be an unbearable burden, but actually, see, I'm just bonding

---

[1] Colic is a common medical condition in babies, defined in the medical literature as "whenever the infant cries uncontrollably for long stretches of time in seeming great pain when there is absolutely nothing wrong."

here with other guys, and I'll include women in that, who love their babies dearly and would jump off a cliff for them, in fact *have* jumped off a cliff, but who need to *vent* about it a little now and then.

The truth is, I love babies. They really put their whole face into everything, and their heart and soul with it. Also, babies keep you honest. You cannot lie to babies, because they don't understand words yet, only actions. You will be amazed at how disconcerting it can be, even for an honest person like yourself, to not be able to use words to, shall we say, reposition someone else's reality. Like you're saying, as you leave the room, "I'll be right back," but the baby only sees you walking away. So in your mind, what's happening already is the joyous return of the parent, while for the baby this scene is all about departure.

Baby Social Skills

If you are a father-to-be, let me help to prepare you for having a baby in the house. Imagine a roommate who has no knowledge of any social conventions and is totally, utterly helpless. She requires you to provide all her meals instantly, half of which she throws up, without warning, in fact usually preceded by a big smile. When old enough, she throws all her food on the floor. Every so often, she pees on you. She can't be left alone, except when sleeping, which she will not do unless you spend a few hours rocking, reading, and singing her to sleep. Not your ideal roommate, unless you love this person beyond all reason. Which, fortunately for her, you do.

Communicating with Your Baby

The big issue with babies, really, is communication, because if you think guys are bad at it, you should see babies. If babies could talk, there really wouldn't be any problem. The baby would just say, "Oh, Dad, do you think you could hold me at about eighty-seven degrees with my head rotated four degrees, held by your left hand with your right leg bouncing while rocking forward and back at a rate of two rocks per second with an intermittent sideways rock of three to four seconds duration at intervals of thirty seconds? Great, now sing ... no, not that one ... well, never mind, I'm ... yawn ... zzzzzzzz."

Of course, this presumes that in addition to being able to talk, babies are totally self-aware, way more than me, let me tell you. My pants could be on fire and I wouldn't know what was bothering me until maybe a few weeks later. "Honey," my wife would say, "it really seems like something's been bothering you these last few weeks." "I'm fine!" I would cheerily snarl. "Does it have anything to do with your pants?" "Pants, what pants?" "The ones you're wearing, the ones that are still smoldering there on the left leg, with the seat all burned out." "There's nothing wrong with these pants, it's just too hot in this room, that's all ... hey, wait a minute! I'm on fire!"

Not to worry, your baby will learn to speak eventually, but not until you've considered private tutoring because your neighbor's children all started talking at four months. Babies first learn words by associating what you say with what they are perceiving. For example, you see a cat and you say "Ooh, look at the kitty!" Or you lift the baby out of the high chair and say "Up we go!" Or you stub your toe and say "@#$%^&*!!!!" If these phrases are repeated often enough, your child will eventually learn to use them correctly, except for the last one, which need only slip out *one* time and the child will begin to use it correctly immediately, which will make quite an impression on his or her grandparents.

Constant Motion

Babies like you to be walking. You can hold the baby in exactly the same position as you carefully sit down, keeping up the rocking motion, and the baby will start to cry as soon as you start to get comfortable. Come on—get up! Walk! You see, babies want to have the upper hand—to keep you on your toes, literally.

There is an important biological reason for this. This is the beginning of a lifelong process of wearing you down so that when they're sixteen and ask for the car keys, you won't have the energy to refuse. The only way you can get your resources back is to get some sleep, which you finally will be able to do, as soon as you get to work.

It's not just being held, it's not just the motion. Perhaps walking motion is more like what they felt in the womb. Bouncing is merely a distraction and is unwomblike, unless the mother did aerobics right through pregnancy. I won't go too far with this womb stuff, since they also may have been upside down in the womb.

So you carry the baby for hours and hours, while it's crying as if *its* pants are on fire, until finally it succumbs to exhaustion and falls asleep. So what do *you* do? Put it down and go take a nap? No! Of course not! Because now is your big chance to really appreciate the sweetness and beauty of your sleeping child, so you carry it for another half an hour just to bask in parental pride and the kind of love that is possible only when there is absolute quiet.

I suspect I'm not alone in this, but I love to dance with sleeping or at least extremely groggy babies. Alert babies would never put up with this—at least mine wouldn't. Any kind of music will do—well, any kind that I listen to now that I no longer have the urge to be in a punk rock band.

The sleep dancing has a slightly different feeling depending on whether it's a father-daughter or father-son thing. With my baby girl I felt like a father must feel dancing with his daughter at her wedding—with my love, the apple of my eye. With my baby boy it was more like just a sweet moment with a baby, and a sharing of rhythm, peace, and harmony.

Of course you can get carried away with the motion thing, too. One time Kayla just would not be comforted. My wife and I both tried. We walked her, we rocked her, we bounced her, we patted her, we spun her, we zoomed her through the air, we ran the 100-meter high hurdles with her, but she only cried more. Finally, in desperation, at wit's end, I just laid her down. She fell asleep, instantly. Duh!

The Baby's Cry

Millions of years of evolution have gone into the design of the baby's cry, to ensure that it is impossible to ignore. Nature has designed the baby's cry to sound like a fire engine on its way to a four-alarmer, only louder and harder to ignore. Or, rather, I should say it is modern engineers who have tried unsuccessfully to emulate this sound in such relatively unalarming devices as the police siren, or the rather ho-hum car alarm.

Making the House Safe for the Baby

The number one hazard to babies in our house was that we tended to lay the baby down just about anywhere, all wrapped up in blankets, looking pretty much like just another pile of stuff. Since we were accustomed to sitting on piles of stuff, for lack of places where there were no piles of stuff, the danger of sitting on the baby was a very real one.

To prevent this from happening you can place a sign on top of the pile. If you have a computer, you can print one—I suggest 144-point type, which is about the size used on a movie marquee. If you don't have a computer, you can hand-letter a sign or buy a premade one from the hardware store, with as appropriate a warning as possible—KEEP OFF THE GRASS might work, or BEWARE OF DOG. I sort of like the one that says INQUIRE WITHIN, because it makes you stop and think.

Your Baby's Development

Your baby is going to develop just fine no matter what you do, so don't worry about it. The main point I would like to make here is, don't try to impress friends with the physical and intellectual accomplishments of your infant. Unless they have children of their own, they will not get it, *at all*.

However, this does not mean that you cannot boast about your child endlessly, nor would I ever suggest that you let any other topic enter the conversation. I simply would advise that when describing your baby's progress, you use internal criteria instead.

For example, don't say "Yeah, he's lifting his head now. I think he's getting ready to roll over." Only people with a child exactly the same age will understand the monumental significance of being able to lift one's head, which in the adult world doesn't seem like a real biggie, unless you're sitting at your desk at about 2:00 in the afternoon and the baby was up all night and so were you and maybe you could just close one eye ...

Also, when your friend learns that your child is lifting it's head, possibly preparing to roll over, one of two things will happen:

Your friend will run to the pediatrician to find out why *his* child is not yet preparing to roll over, or

Your friend will inform you that his child is crossing his hands at midline ... isn't yours?

No, focus on internal criteria instead. Say something like, "He's deeply contemplative, yet enjoys being physical at times." No one can argue with this, and it's something everyone can relate to on their own level.

Also, don't say, "He seems to use most of his energy trying to make a doo-dee in his diaper." Never lie, just keep the conversation at a higher level. Say instead, "He's totally present in his body at this point, totally aware of what he's feeling."

It sounds a whole lot more impressive than telling someone that your baby has found her thumb. Never lie, just keep it at a higher level. While this in fact can be one of the most exciting events of parenthood—since a baby cannot cry and suck its thumb at the same time—it does not exactly make your kid sound like Ivy League material, if you know what I mean.

The Second Child

When we had our second child, one kind friend brought not only a baby present but a whole bag full of little presents for the sibling. This was perhaps the most brilliant human insight since the discovery of gummy worms.

Of course, we're careful about showing affection through *things*, now aren't we? Er, yes, of course. We would never want her to think that toys are in any way being offered as a replacement for her loss of an exclusive relationship with her parents, or that emotional processing should be avoided by means of external distraction. Candy works, too.

You can't try to compare the development of siblings, I know, but at thirteen weeks Kayla had rolled over. At fifteen weeks, Jacob wasn't even close. Can you believe the *Yellow Pages* have no listing for "Tutors, Rolling Over"?

One thing they don't prepare you for in the parenting books is how your own feelings are affected by these major life events. The birth of our second child brought with it, for me, a sadness about the end of our first child's babyhood and empathy for the dramatic change in her life. And, the passing of her infancy had implications for me, too, as I approached forty. Fortunately, sleep deprivation and dirty dishes pretty well take care of any tendency to sit and ponder this, or anything else, for too long.

The best thing about having a second child is that it makes dealing with one child seem like a piece of cake. Things are relatively easier with the second child, though, since you know what you're doing and you have already renounced all worldly desires. In fact, I suggest having your second child first.

Chapter Quiz: The Baby

Here's your chance to test what you have learned in this chapter. In order to control your ego, assume all your answers are wrong.

1. When the baby is crying, you should:
   a. Burp the baby.
   b. Burp to amuse the baby.
   c. Pretend to be a strong, virile he-man who—hey, gotta hand it to you women—doesn't know the first thing about babies.

2. When your friends tell you their three-month-old baby is starting to crawl, you should:
   a. Point out that worms crawl from birth.
   b. Point out that they are liars.
   c. Burp to amuse your friends.
   d. Look in the *Yellow Pages* under "Tutors, Crawling."

CHAPTER 4

The New You

When you have your first child you go from being, well, you, to being someone's father. You are now defined by your relationship to someone else, and frankly no one much cares about who *you* are anymore.

You may also be going from being in a relationship with one significant other to being in a relationship with two others, who are both quite significant, which is geometrically more complicated. (Or is it logarithmically?) While these new relationship states might appear obvious, they really can take you by surprise, especially if you are as emotionally savvy as most of us guys.

Who Am I?

Having a child made me reflect about my own identity, which is a big job for me, being someone who is many different people at once, most of whom don't agree with each other.

While my wife was pregnant with our first child, I grew a beard, figuring that if she was going to be doing the big-time female thing, I ought to do something masculine. About the only definitely male thing I could think of to do, other than the thing which got her into this very female state in the first place, was to grow hair on my face, which actually is not something you do, it's really about *not* doing something. Since I hated shaving anyway, it was a no-brainer. This was a good choice as it turns out, since I no longer would have time to shave even if I wanted to.

Who Is This?

Of course the baby is starting on a quest for identity, too, probably not helped by the fact that, in Jacob's case, I called him either Jason or Nathan for at least three months. This may be why (since everything your child does is your fault), as a three-year-old, the poor kid was really searching hard for an identity, and at any given moment it could be fairly hazardous to venture a guess about who he might be at that moment. He and Kayla frequently had exchanges like this one:

Kayla: Hey, Jacob.
Jacob (angrily): I'M NOT JACOB!!!
Kayla: Hey, Batman.
Jacob (more angrily): I'M NOT BATMAN!!!
Kayla: Hey, Robin.
Jacob (totally, totally normally): What?

She was lucky to have gotten it on the third try. Other choices included the Green Power Ranger, the Red Power Ranger, the Blue Power Ranger, the White Power Ranger, and so on.

What the New You Looks Like

One nice thing is that you're not alone in being a father. The world is full of new fathers and fathers of young children, and they are pretty easy to pick out. In case you would like to find another one to do some bonding with, without admitting it of course, here's a guide.

How to recognize a new father:
- Bags under eyes
- Has a cold
- Has milky spots on his shirt, particularly in the shoulder area
- Top button is in the second button hole, and so on down the line

- Mismatched socks
- Mismatched shoes
- Mismatched, or only one, glove[2]

How to recognize a father of young children:
- Dinosaur stickers on his pants legs
- Food on his pants legs
- Food on his shirt
- Food in his hair
- Hair is uncombed
- Eats food that others have dropped
- Eats dinosaur stickers
- Moves everyone's full juice glasses away from the edge of the table
- Spills his own juice

Family Roles

By virtue of your position as a father, there are certain duties incumbent upon you, dictated by the offspring themselves.

For example, when Kayla was about three, whenever I would correct her, she then insisted that I make a similar mistake so she could correct me. "Point to that (an elephant) and call it a walrus, daddy." I would point. I would call it a walrus. "NO, that's an ELEPHANT!" she would note with glee.

But my job was to call it a walrus, because I knew from then on she'd remember which one was the walrus and because we could share a laugh, laughing at both of us really, for being

---

[2]A benign mismatch is when they are different styles/colors but there is one for each hand; a fatal mismatch is when both gloves are for the same hand, in which case one gloved hand appears to be rotated 180 degrees on the arm.

human and making mistakes. I showed her that I can make mistakes too, and it's all right. Either that or I was teaching her to humiliate those who are wiser to make herself look smarter, thereby encouraging her to become a little tyrant. But I don't think so.

Then there was: "Be quiet while I read, Daddy." (I *never* said that to her.) This from a *three-year-old* who was claiming she needed to *read*. So she would start to fake-read, and then she'd say, "Now you talk while I'm reading and I'll tell you to be quiet."

So my job was to talk. "Blah, blah, blah," I would say, accommodatingly.

"Daddy! Now do you want me to read or do you want to take a time out?"

No one ever said that to *her*! In addition to repeating what you say, children repeat what you don't say, I swear.

By the way, time outs are a great new child-rearing innovation, and have even been written up in that great source of sensitive parenting advice, the *Wall Street Journal*. I guess they can relate—a time out is basically what you get on Wall Street if you bilk investors out of millions.

So anyway, everyone in the family has a job to do. The job of a baby is to digest milk, and he takes this very seriously. He will work into the wee small hours of the morning to get it done. Your job in this case is to help the baby digest his milk, which is kind of like helping someone else to breathe. But still, it's your job and if you don't at least try, the child welfare people will show up with handcuffs.

The work of an infant (a crawler) is to try to kill himself, with your job being, of course, to stop him. He gets extra points if you are only two inches away at the time of his demise but still somehow cannot prevent the catastrophe. You get extra points if you were upstairs in the bathroom when you sensed the air vibrations and dived down an entire flight of stairs, without your feet ever touching down, to catch the étagère as it toppled toward him. You get super bonus points if you catch any of the falling tchotchkes as you save your child.

The job of a two-year-old is to run the entire world, a demanding job which understandably leads to periods of great frustration. At these times it often becomes necessary to lie on the floor, kicking and pounding fists and screaming. Sometimes the *child* will do this, too. Your job is to keep your name off of the police blotter.

In general, your job, throughout your children's childhood, is to do it again. Whatever it was you just did—built a tower of blocks, helped with a puzzle, read a book, tossed a child into the air, swung a child by her ankles, ran 100 meters in 9.9 seconds with a child on your head. You are exhausted, brain-dead, breathless, and probably wet for any of a number of reasons. But you do it again. Only *faster* this time, Daddy! *Higher*, Daddy! *Really* high this time. Really *really* high. And then again, and again, and again, until you are willing to give in and let her have a lollipop as a diversion.

That is your job, Daddy. Build it again, Daddy. And this time make it really, *really* big. And call it a walrus.

Chapter Quiz: The New You

Did you actually read this chapter or are you one of those wise-guys who thinks that if he can pass the quiz he doesn't need to read the chapter? I hope you're the latter because having read this chapter will be of absolutely no use in this quiz.

1. Your role as a father is to:
   a. Develop a new sense of yourself in terms of your relationship to your new child.
   b. Be a role model by not acting out in the way that you usually do, which would make your infant appear mature by comparison.
   c. Learn to say "Barney" without preceding it with any colorful adjectives, and I don't mean purple.
   d. Burp to amuse your wife.

CHAPTER 5

The Courage to Change— Diapers, That Is

A whole chapter on diapers? Yes, I do feel it is warranted only because this seems to be of major concern to new dads. Sure you'll work six jobs so the kid can go to Yale, sure you'd face Godzilla in your pajamas to protect your child, but ... diapers? Like, touch them? No way!

Okay, just get over it. Yes, you are going to have to change diapers. Yes, they will be what we refer to in polite society as "soiled." No, this has nothing to do with soil, as in dirt, or gardening, or farming, other than a certain connection to fertilizer. It's like this: Fish gotta swim, birds gotta fly, babies gotta go when they gotta go and—perhaps this is the part you have trouble with—the female of the species can no longer be relied on to shoulder the entire infant waste management function in society. Sorry about that, but socioeconomic cultural-historical anthropological forces, you see. Don't worry, you get used to it, sort of.

Believe it or not, and I'll try not to get overly sentimental here since this is a book for guys, diaper changing can actually be a tender time. For some reason, my son always grinned like the Cheshire cat during diaper changes. It's either because he was so happy to have my undivided, face-to-face attention, or because he knew he was about to shoot a stream of pee into my eye.

The hard part, oddly enough, is not the act of diapering itself but the mental stress of the decisions required in the diaper procurement process.

Cloth or Plastic?

There is quite a debate about whether one should use cloth or plastic diapers. The plastic diaper companies, in a remarkable display of corporate citizenship and environmental concern, have done extensive research and found that, guess what, using plastic diapers is the best environmental choice after all! It was *so* nice of them to find that out for us. I'll bet they would have been real disappointed if their careful research had shown just the opposite.

My environmental advice is, use cloth. However, I personally did not take this advice, so, I guess, do what you want. It's a lifestyle choice, and I believe plastic diapers are a choice that is okay even with the radical right. Actually, we did use cloth for a year. This involved a lifestyle where we felt good about our stewardship of the planet's resources and limited disposal space. We made hiney wipes out of cut-up pieces of old baby blankets (that we stole from the hospital, as did you). We kept a thermos of lukewarm water handy in which to wet them so we wouldn't have to run the tap water for five minutes until it got warm.

We then decided to switch to a lifestyle where we felt good about the way the bathroom smelled, since the diaper service came only once a week and by then, let me tell you, the hamper basically turns into an oven that warms and slowly cooks the yummies inside. There were other reasons, too. Excuse me while I get some air.

The transition happened like this. At first we used cloth all the time, and when we went somewhere with the baby we would bring along extra diapers and plastic bags to keep the used ones in until we got home. When we got home, we would then leave the baby bag in the kitchen until the next time we went out, two weeks later, and guess what? There was that bag with the poopy diaper, two weeks later, looking like a science project gone out of control. It was so gross we had to wash it—separately, twice—before even returning it to the diaper service for laundering.

So then we started to say, okay, we'll buy some plastic diapers to use when we go out somewhere. So before an outing we would change from cloth to plastic. At first we felt pretty guilty about just throwing them away. Then we started saying, gee, we'd better put her in plastic because we *might* go out later. Then, gee, the plastic seems to work better at nighttime. You get the drift. One word: Plastics[3].

So if you must use plastic, at least send a check to the Sierra Club. And if you also use a "Diaper Genie" (the device that shrink-wraps used plastic diapers in more plastic before you dispose of them in plastic garbage bags), say six Hail Marys and send a check to Greenpeace as well.

Buying Diapers with Only a College Education

So, like I said, diapering is no big deal. It's *buying* them that fills me with fear.

Warning! If you have never purchased diapers ... pay attention, there's going to be a quiz on this. The pink packages are for girls. The blue ones are for boys and are, presumably, a little roomier in the front. It's important to remember the sex of your child when buying diapers, although it can be difficult to remember even the location of your own appendages when faced with a display of diaper packages twenty feet high and the length of the Great Wall of China.

The Ultras, while thinner and thus more fashionable (especially when wearing hip-hugger denims), are treated with chemicals. To be avoided, some say, which is enough for me. I don't want my pure and perfect child coming into contact with chemicals of any kind until she's working on her Ph.D. in microbiology.

---

[3]This is a cultural reference. If you don't get it, you are obviously culturally illiterate and never saw Dustin Hoffman in *The Graduate*.

Then you must select the size, which is identified in three ways:

1) By a code number (1, 2, 3, etc.) which in no way corresponds to your child's age, shoe size, or anything else;

2) By a descriptor such as crawler, toddler, walker, 500-meter hurdler, and so on, which is totally useless because small children often walk sooner than big children, so mobility actually would be *inversely* related to diaper size; or

3) By a weight range, which is the only helpful one. Unfortunately, we never weigh our children so I have no idea how much they weigh. Plus, the ranges seem to be totally random, like the three sizes might be: 6 lbs. to 47 lbs., 22 lbs. to 31 lbs., or 16 lbs. to 39 lbs.

My rule is, if you can find one labeled medium, which you may find on alternate Thursdays, nab it. Otherwise always buy size 2, and work with it.

If you do somehow figure out your child's diaper size, try very hard to memorize it, so you can ask the clerk if they might have any more in the stock room since they are totally out of them on the floor. I like to stick with the smaller size for as long as possible since you get more for the same price and it's that much less for the landfill. My children have very narrow hips for this reason. I do have my limits: When derrière cleavage starts to show, or the child turns blue, it's time for the next size.

Diapernomics

Financial management tip: The store brand diapers are the cheapest, but they are usually out of stock ... in your size. Do not buy ten boxes of the next bigger size when they are on sale, for your child to grow into. Your child will toilet train prematurely if he finds this out.

How many diapers will you need? Most first-time parents will buy forty or fifty packages of newborn-size diapers just to be on the safe side. Unfortunately, the baby, if fed, will outgrow this size within hours of birth. This is perhaps why many parents go on to have second and third children. If you see a family of six or seven, you can bet they overbought on the newborn diapers, big time.

The average newborn requires a diaper change approximately every two days, by my standards, or, if a responsible adult is present, and I really don't want to pick on mothers-in-law here, about every twelve minutes. Therefore, in a twenty-four-hour period, you will need somewhere between one-half and one-hundred-and-twenty diapers. A diaper costs about fifty cents, so a little quick math here and you will calculate that ... okay, I'll give you a little more time for the math ... that's right, diapers will cost you about $18,000 per year. Plus Wet-Wipes.

Don't worry, you won't have to change diapers for the rest of your life. Eventually you will get to do toilet training. Unfortunately for you, it will come years after your mother-in-law believes it should have. Her children were toilet trained at 6 months (see also the chapters on Truth and Mothers-in-Law).

Diaper Management Techniques

Here are some helpful hints relating to diaper management.

My wife and I have learned not to say things in public like "*Sniff, sniff* I think *some*body has a poopy diaper!" This saves the other one the embarrassment of having to say, "Er, uh, it's not *her*, dear *blush, blush*."

Actually if you want to have some fun at a party with families, just quietly pass a little gas and watch twenty kids get their diapers changed.

You know a diaper has been on too long if it is so heavy that it breaks through the bottom of the trash can when you throw it away, crashes through the bathroom floor, and lands in the living room. If it also goes through the living room floor, you *really* should have changed it earlier.

Here's an important bit of practical diapering advice if you have a man-child. Point it down, into the diaper. Otherwise, a stream shoots up out of the diaper and hits him in the chin, or at the very least sends his outfit to the laundry pile, which is already the size of Mount Rushmore. I felt very New Dad-ish when I passed this bit of advice on to my wife. "You mean it *stays* down?" she said, doubtfully. "If you make the diaper tight enough, it does," I replied. I learned early on that it's nearly impossible to make a diaper too tight, even though with my first child I spent the entire first year thinking that maybe her diaper was too tight, since there was no other apparent reason for her obviously great distress.

The Zen of Diapering

Life is change, yet I often find I'm resisting life by resisting change. That intimate, personal revelation will, I'm sure, make sales of this book skyrocket. One could also conclude that life is changing diapers, and one would not be wrong—no, indeed. One probably also hasn't had enough sleep, but that's another chapter.

Brian Eno, in *Oblique Strategies*, offers the oracular wisdom that "Repetition is a form of change." Think about it. With every diaper change you are a different person when you have finished than you were when you started. Just a little. But it's the little changes that add up and get you.

Chapter Quiz: Diapers

Never mind, no quiz here. Just lab work. Go to it, Dad!

CHAPTER 6

The Zen of Stuff

The sacred and spiritual advent of the birth of a baby kindles the fires of love in the human heart and awakens the natural desire in friends and family to fill the new child's surroundings with mountains and mountains of *stuff*, mostly plastic. Oh, there's still the occasional eccentric who will buy a wooden toy (usually someone who frequents Appalachian craft fairs), and this is the toy you will strategically place on the toy shelf as a testament to the sophistication of your tastes and the level of refinement to which your child will be heir. But for the most part it will be plastic, trust me.

Someday I'm going to start a mail order company just to sell all the things we accumulated in the first three years of familyhood. My catalog will include:

Swingomatic

The next best thing to Daddy's arms for rocking baby to sleep, but now Daddy can take out the trash and pay the bills while Junior nods off, powerless to resist the magic of motion. We hate to part with this one but it's just not big enough for teenagers. Runs on two "D" batteries. Replace batteries every fifteen minutes for maximum effect. Two settings, but don't bother with low—go with warp speed. Available while supply lasts. We have only twenty-seven—one for every room in the house, plus spares in the basement and attic.

Play-Doh

Parental vigilance has kept color cross-contamination to ten percent or less, except for the fluorescent lime. Glow-in-the-dark colors add a nice accent to any carpet.

Sesame Street Play Gym

Just the kind of large plastic primary-colored gizmo you swore you would never allow in the house. Until, that is, seven different aunts, uncles, and officemates all simultaneously and separately (probably during a cosmic convergence) had the inspiration to buy you one. Those who felt they wanted to spend a little extra money regardless of the torture it would inflict on you bought the battery-operated version, in which Big Bird tosses a fake Ping Pong ball back and forth (whirrrrrr-*blonk!* whirrrrrr-*blonk!*), and a computer chip blasts out a rendition of "Somewhere Over the Rainbow" that will so thoroughly pierce your ears you'll be able to wear every earring in your wife's collection at the same time (in your eardrum, of course). Unfortunately, kids love this toy. If you try to put it away they will find the box and make you reassemble it. However, remember, you are the parent and you have a right to hide the batteries.

Personally, I do not find these toys intellectually stimulating. I always looked forward to when the children would be older and we could start buying something that I as an adult could be challenged by, like Rock-'Em Sock-'Em Robots.

Clothes

Here is an important infant fashion tip: all clothes for children of diapering age must have snaps up one leg and down the other. Never buy clothes that do not have this feature. Also, the top should have snaps all the way down the front. The snaps should never be down the back—what sadistic maniac thinks you are going to change your baby while he's face down? The general idea is that the garment should be capable of being unsnapped to the point where it completely falls away so you don't have to throw the baby around too much during a diaper change. This is especially important when undertaking the very delicate "sleeping diaper change," or the incredible "nursing diaper change."

Books

We are very careful about the books we allow our children to read, especially since they can't read yet and so we are the ones who have to do the reading. There really are a lot of children's books that are totally S-T-U-P-I-D, if you know what I mean.

While we are stalwart defenders of the First Amendment, we fully utilize our powers of parental censorship. We have instituted a tiered system of censorship, in which there are three levels:

1) Books that we bury in the back of the bookshelf because we don't ever want to have to read them. These are the S-T-U-P-I-D books.

2) Books that go to Goodwill because not only don't we ever want to read them, we don't want anyone else reading them to our children either. These are mostly books with dubious messages, although I feel we allow a lot of leeway here. After all, we have allowed your basic *Snow White* and *Cinderella* stories to infiltrate, which certainly have dubious messages: If you spend your life naively taking care of slovenly and not-too-bright men or cunning, mean-spirited women, eventually a rich handsome prince whom you don't even really know will swoop down out of nowhere and then, *vôilà*, you suddenly will be happy, whatever that means. Women spend years in therapy trying to undo the damage of these stories, each of which I have read to my daughter at least 500 times, no exaggeration. Still, I have to admit that I consider the Disney *Snow White* movie to be a true masterpiece, which shows what happens to your aesthetic sensibilities after a few years of parenthood.

3) Then there are books that go directly (and usually, I confess, clandestinely) into the recycling because we would not wish these books on anyone in the world, parent or child. This can backfire. I had completely disassembled one book (the cover had to be removed to go in with glossy paper, while the inside

went with white paper—we try to be environmentally correct about these things), when my daughter insisted on reading it. I had hoped she would forget about this newly arrived present amidst the other newly arrived presents, but this girl has a mind like a steel trap. So I had to tape it back together and read it about ten times. Just to give you an idea of where I'm coming from on this stuff, this was a book about a Mr. Blabbermouth, who went on and on endlessly about nothing—that is the whole point of this book, how annoying he was to everyone because he went on and on and on about nothing—and *all his blabbering is rendered verbatim in the book.* What sort of a mind would write such a book?

Here is a helpful tip when looking for books to read to your child. The best ones have certain key words in the title that indicate they have a fine literary sensibility that you will want to pass on to your child. These words include "sleep," "sleepy," "quiet," "night," and "bedtime" (see also the chapter on Sleep). Yes, books can help to induce a restful state, and if they don't, well, there's always the rubber mallet.

Child Management Devices

The Swingomatic

I know I already talked about it, but I just can't say enough about the Swingomatic. In fact, remind me to send a thank you note to the manufacturer. We didn't buy one for our first child, feeling that a child should be held, nurtured, touched, not left to swing alone in some mechanical device. Which is all very true, but when the second child came along there was now one child apiece, and if we were both spending all our time touching children, no one could make dinner, which is not really a tenable situation. Buy one, or borrow one, or come get one of mine. Get fresh batteries so it swings real fast. Babies like that.

The Child Harness

One friend gave us a child harness, designed to allow you to take your little one with you to Macy's on the day after Thanksgiving. I don't like to use it for the same reason I don't like to put our cats on a leash. If you've ever tried to walk a cat on a leash you'll know what I mean, especially if you've tried it in a shopping mall. Plus if you put a kid in a harness, his goal in life becomes to break free and run, which will be really dangerous when he hits the teen years.

The Snuggly

These hold the baby close to your body, but there is one important piece of advice for Snuggly use which I learned the hard way: The child must be actually *in* the device before you let go of him or he will go plummeting to the floor. They should have warning labels to this effect.

The best way to select a baby-carrying device is to listen to the advice of twenty or thirty other people who have used them and then pick something different. It is such a highly personalized choice that, in America, there exist approximately 3.7 baby-carrying device styles for each and every parent.

Toys

Of 800 stuffed animals in the house, the only one in the bedroom at 3:00 in the morning, when Kayla insists on having something to cuddle with, is the froggie that croaks when moved. So here's an important pointer: no toys that make noise in the bedroom. Preferably, no toys that make noise at all. Remember, toys have a way of realizing their full potential at the most inopportune moments.

Special warning: Beware of the talking ball that makes an animal sound, then says the name of the animal, whenever it is moved. It can be moved by a child exploring sounds and words, it can be moved by an adult trying to carry a sleeping child to bed in a dark room, and occasionally it can be moved by the rotation of the earth or the settling of your house. The killer is that—and this is what convinced me that this toy was designed by a sadist—about ten seconds after you walk away from the ball and breathe a sigh of relief that all is quiet and the sleeping child hasn't awakened, the ball pipes up and says, "Good-bye!" Arrghh! The child wakes up, you say words that your child will later repeat in front of her grandparents, and the ball then becomes quiet, until the cat walks by it at 2 a.m.

You, like me, may be led to ponder: Just how important *is* it that my child learn all the animal noises before the age of two, and could there be some other way to learn them? Silly you. Animal sound recognition and imitation is an important skill that will serve your child well later in life, like in eigth grade when he needs to imitate the school principal by make hog-snorting noises.

The Stuff Continuum

If your extended family is large enough you will never have to buy clothes or toys for your child. It is a myth that these are the expenses of having children. All children's clothes and toys are received as presents, so it is the rest of the world that decides what your children will own. You will instead be buying for other children what you wish people would buy for you. This is why Goodwill, the Salvation Army, and consignment shops are thriving. These are also excellent places to shop.

Chapter Quiz: Things

Are you still paying attention? We'll soon find out. If you answer all these questions correctly, you win a talking animal sounds ball.

1. S-T-U-P-I-D spells:
   a. The Goodwill store.
   b. The recycling center.
   c. The dump.
   d. Any of the above.

2. It is important to control the accumulation of things in your house because:
   a. You do not want to clog your psychic channels.
   b. You do not want your children to equate happiness with possessions.
   c. You do not want your children to become hollow, materialistic shells.
   d. You do not want your children to become lost in the clutter.

3. All good children's books end with:
   a. "The End."
   b. "And they all lived happily ever after."
   c. Everyone falling asleep.
   d. The Goodwill store.

CHAPTER 7

Got the Time?

Does Anybody Really Know What Time It Is?

Time is an abstract concept that even adults don't fully appreciate, especially in my house, as I will demonstrate a little later, if I have time. Toddlers try really hard to get a handle on it, but basically they are totally clueless about whether a person is leaving for five minutes or forever.

Children live in the moment. For a two-year-old there is only the Now and the Not Now, and anything other than Now is, let's face it, not really happening and is therefore unacceptable. One of my favorite time-warp mind-benders was when Kayla would say, "When I used to be bigger I used to ..." Words like "yesterday," "last night," or "last month" all mean the same thing, as do "tomorrow," "later," and "September." All mean Not Now.

Toddlers basically figure that all this time stuff is an adult fabrication, so they're right at home with it—making things up is their whole shtick—and are happy to join the game. Like, we're always saying, "You can do that when you're older," to which Kayla responds, "I'm older already." Our semantics around time are so limited that even a toddler can get around them.

Being in the Moment

I don't like to use the term "baby-sitting" to refer to my time with the kids. When I do, it's for purely vindictive reasons, as in "No, I didn't change the cat litter, I've been *baby-sitting* for the last three hours while *you* ..." As if I had been sentenced to the most horrible of fates.

I have to remember, this is my life, right now, this moment. My children will never be this age again. This is my life, happening right now, so I'd best be enjoying it. What else am I going to do, change the cat litter?

How to Get Places on Time

Because I enjoy suffering for the environment, I wash and reuse my plastic baggies and, for a long time, refused to buy a second car. Both of these practices saved money, as most environmentally conscious practices do. I had to give in on the car issue, though. It all started the day I lost my daughter's peanut butter and jelly sandwich, causing me to miss the train.

You see, I take a commuter train to work, so in a one-car family that meant that my wife, and therefore the whole family, had to give me a ride to the station on mornings when it was too nasty outside to ride my bike there. On these days, in a one-car family, in order to catch the 8:23 train I had to rise at about 4 a.m., get myself ready, get my daughter up, dressed, fed, and into the car, along with wife and baby. The last straw was when I lost the baggie with Kayla's peanut butter and jelly sandwich in it while running around with the baby looking for his car seat, which we bring into the house as a carrier and hide in various rooms the night before.

Kayla was, of course, upset at the loss of her breakfast (we *never* give her peanut butter and jelly for breakfast, *never,* I swear it was just this one time), and my great guilt over this caused me to look one last time where I knew it wasn't because I had already looked there twice. To my great dismay, it still wasn't there, and of course I missed the train by seconds. Even though I remembered that the south-bound train would be on the north-bound track due to repairs. Even though the 8:23 is the express and if I miss it, I miss my vanpool on the other end, as well as the bus, so I either wait an hour for the next bus or pay $8.00 for a cab, which kills me. And I get to work late. And I've been up for five hours.

Another reason we missed the train that day, I'm convinced, is that someone set the car clock to the correct time. The car clock must be at least two minutes fast at all times or our ability to function in the real world is destroyed. And the kitchen clock must be five minutes fast. The bedroom clock, of course, must be fifteen minutes fast[4].

This clever manipulation of time takes the place of intravenous injections of adrenaline. A big shot when the alarm goes off ("Good Lord, it's already 7 a.m.! I should have been out of bed fifteen minutes ago!"). Then another milder shot to counteract breakfast complacency ("8:05?! We should be heading out the door! Has the baby nursed on both sides yet? Where are Kayla's shoes/coat/hat/book/pants/peanut butter and jelly sandwich?").

These clocks squeeze us out the door, and the car clock adds that edge that gets us there ("Hurry it up! The train leaves in five minutes!").

But wait, you say. Shouldn't a couple of college graduates figure out that the bedroom clock is fast and say, "Oh goody, it's really only 6:45, not 7:00"? Or, set the clock to the right time and learn that at 6:45 you *must* get up? Ha! No! We tried setting the clocks to the right time once and missed the train three days in a row. And we have *Master's* degrees!

Since this is meant to be a helpful book, I was going to name this chapter "Time Management." "Ha, ha, ha," I thought, "What a funny title!" "Time Out of Control" would be more like it.

I'd like to say that having kids forced us to fool ourselves with the clocks. I'd *like* to say that, but actually we've always done this. Now our children will have to as well, because they too will think it's possible to make a seven minute drive to a train station in two minutes.

---

[4]That was true when I started writing this book. We now keep the bedroom clock twenty-five minutes fast. You think I'm kidding?

Measuring Time

Remember, life is measured in weeks for the first three months, then you switch to months, until your child is age two at which point you use years. At fifty you can use half-centuries.

It all has to do with the rate of change, which is sort of like acceleration. You only get to use weeks and months again if you go through changes at an accelerated rate at some point in your life, such as if you give up drinking. This is such an accelerated change that for the first three months of sobriety you use days, not weeks, as a measurement. After ninety days, you revert to months, then after one year you go back to years. If you plan to give up drinking I highly recommend that you do it before having children. Having two members of the family accelerating at the same time could lead to a high-speed collision.

Prioritizing Your Time

These are some of the prioritizing decisions I face when everyone else is napping and isn't expected to wake up for ten more minutes—should I:

- Shave and trim my beard (this may be my only chance before Christmas, since it's already October)?
- Fix that leak (before the sun deck rots and collapses onto the patio)?
- Do a backup of our computer databases before our semiannual hard disk failure?
- Touch up the shutters (so the neighbors don't think we're lowering property values)?
- Go to the bathroom (for obvious reasons—besides, if I don't go I might be setting myself up for prostate problems later in life)?
- Eat lunch (to avoid debilitating headaches)?
- Work on this book? (Nah, forget it.)

Oops—there's the baby ...

The Dead Mouse Time Prioritization System

Dead mice have to wait. As a parent I have to attend to whatever is most pressing, and I constantly assess not only the current environment but my own value system. For example, if someone reports that the cat has brought a mouse into the house, I will ask, "Is it dead or alive?" If dead, it will have to wait. There are too many living things clamoring for my attention for me to give priority to a dead one, with all due respect to the former mouse.

If it were still alive, I would do my best to save it, although it seems somewhat pointless to save a mouse that the cat actually caught and then feed the cat a can of cow kidney.

My prioritization system is roughly as follows, in descending order of importance:

1. Living human screaming
2. Living nonhuman screaming
3. Living nonhuman in the cat's mouth, in the house
4. Living human whining
5. Living nonhuman, loose in the house
6. Dead nonhuman in the house, near the baby
7. Dead nonhuman on the patio

Don't worry—if it appears there is a dead *human* in the house or on the patio, it is probably just a sleep-deprived parent.

Take a good look inside at your own value system and devise your own priority hierarchy. You could add inanimate objects to this list, such as a stack of dishes about to hit the floor or a lamp about to be rammed with a tricycle (how did *that* get into the house—lamps are supposed to be on the patio where they'll be safe).

I, however, go on a case-by-case basis as far as prioritization goes, since my concern for material possessions varies greatly. There are days when I would drop the screaming baby to save the toppling dishes, and days when I would knock the dishes over myself and then dance on the broken pieces, just to teach them a lesson.

So I hope this insight into my decision-making process will help you in prioritizing your own time. If you have any suggestions on this topic, please feel free to write ... when you have the chance.

Chapter Quiz: Time

You have two hours to complete this quiz. Ready? Begin. Oops—there's the phone, you'd better get it, and by the way, a small person just dropped a houseplant into the toilet. Did I mention the baby's diaper?

1. In order to get places on time now that you have kids, you must:
   a. Think ahead and allow the necessary time for getting everyone ready, allowing extra time for special contingencies.
   b. Drag children out of the house unfed and naked if necessary, to show that you mean business when you say it's time to go.
   c. Explain the importance of punctuality and ask for cooperation. Have the family repeat the affirmation "I always get places on time, easily and effortlessly."
   d. Set your clocks fifteen minutes fast and count on being late most of the time anyway.

CHAPTER 8

To Sleep or Not to Sleep

"To sleep, perchance to dream ..."

Hamlet seemed to assume that anyone could go to sleep whenever they wanted to, and the only thing in question would be whether or not they would dream. Hamlet clearly did not have small children.

If you haven't had a baby yet, here's what to expect. Let's say you now sleep eight hours and live your life in the other sixteen. Okay. Now, prepare to do some math here. Taking care of a child requires approximately seventeen-and-a-half hours a day. So how many hours are left? Okay, okay, that was hard. Let's just assume that you have eight hours left and are free to either sleep or live your life, as you choose.

You can get things done while the baby is sleeping but it's a bargain with the devil. Just when she wakes up, you suddenly realize—but wait, I'm exhausted, I can't possibly function without a nap! But it's too late. You've traded away your sleep for a little of what you still think of as normal life—being able to do the laundry, take out the garbage, pay the bills, go to the bathroom. Maybe you even recklessly read a magazine or had a cup of tea. Oh well, you can always catch up on your sleep later, when everyone else is asleep at the same time again. Like, between 3:39 and 4:07 a.m.

Pleasant dreams.

Sleep Management Techniques

There are two types of people for whom sleep is important: Type X: often referred to as babies, infants, or toddlers.
Type Y: parents.

The Type X people must be asleep in order for the Type Y people to get to sleep. Therefore if you are a Y, you might want to use some of the following methods to get the X's to sleep:

Methods of Getting the Baby to Sleep

Shake and Bake	Keep baby in constant motion, after having wrapped it in forty-seven blankets and several knit caps.
Get It Loaded	No, no, no, on breast milk or formula!
Rubber Mallet	Ha! Ha! You know me—always kidding around.

If all else fails, *grab the car keys*. It won't take long before you start calling your car the Sleep-O-Matic. It's an invaluable tool for nap management, when used correctly. Disadvantage: there's only so much napping *you* can do while driving.

Nocturnal Negotiations

Here is a typical conversation my wife and I would have at—what time was it?

Wife: "Here, he's nursed. I don't know why he's crying. Put him on your chest."

Me: "I tried that, he doesn't want that."

Wife: "Well then, get up and walk around with him."

Me: "Oh, sure, make *me* get up."

Let me tell you, maybe Mother Teresa was gracious when awakened in the middle of the night, but I am probably still a few reincarnations away from sainthood. Unfortunately for me, by the time my wife wakes me up to take over baby-care, she has pretty much already come to the conclusion that it is, in fact, my turn. I, however, am still in the fact-finding phase. As any congressperson can tell you, there is no better stalling technique than a fact-finding phase. While the facts do generally bear out her conclusion, I feel that I am within my rights to, uh, try to see if there's any way I can weasel out of having to get up.

Oh well, it's amazing what you can get done when one of your little loved ones wakes you up at 5 a.m. He may go back to sleep at 5:15, but you are now awake for the day.

The worst part isn't being wakened ten times a night, it's not being able to get back to sleep because some idiotic ditty like "Miss Lucy Had a Baby" keeps going through your head.

A Modest Proposal

The only time you stand a chance of getting some extra sleep is when daylight saving time ends and the clocks are set back an hour. Since infants and toddlers can't read clocks, their plan to make you get up at 5 a.m. is foiled because it is actually 6 a.m. at what used to be 5 a.m. and you have gotten an extra hour of sleep.

Therefore, I propose we do this every day. Every night at 10 p.m. (or whenever the children fall asleep) we set the clocks back one hour. This would in effect give us a twenty-five-hour day—who wouldn't want that?

The Family Bed

Because we prefer to do everything differently from everyone else in western civilization, our family practices the concept known as "The Family Bed." This means, yes, that everyone sleeps in the same bed, at least while the kids are little. We're estimating five years. When we tell people this, they always say, "Oh that must be really nice," but what they're really thinking is, "How utterly weird. I shall have to remember to report you to Family Services."

Actually the family bed has been one of the most rewarding experiences of my life, surpassing even the time I scored under par in miniature golf.

Let me address some of the FAQs (frequently asked questions) about the family bed.

Why did you decide to do a family bed?

It all started at the baby stage. My wife figured, why get up six times in the middle of the night to go nurse the baby when she could just roll over and do it? And she nursed for about two years. By that point we were kind of used to it. It's really quite wonderful having the little cuddly things right there.

Doesn't it get kind of crowded?

It works like this in a family bed: The larger you are, the less space you are allotted, and vice versa. This isn't really a problem, unless you are trying to sleep.

Aren't you afraid you'll roll over on them and, well, smoosh them?

Many people underestimate the size of a child. Try putting a smallish watermelon in your bed and then see how easy it is to roll on top of it.

Don't you need some privacy?

Parents? Have privacy? Look at it this way, all little kids come into their parents' bedrooms anyway, and you never know when they're going to burst in. At least with them right there, we can see for sure when they're asleep.

What we mean is, how can you have sex without waking them up?

My, aren't we nosy? Well, I suppose this book will sell better if I talk about sex, so I'll have to answer that. We normally are bound and gagged when we have sex, so noise isn't a problem. Oooh, this book is going to sell like hotcakes.

What do you do when a child throws up at night in a bed full of people?

When a child is sick, we place a stack of ten towels on each side of the bed in hopes of catching the lasagna vomit in mid-air. Well, so much for book sales.

When the kids move to their own beds, I'm the one who's going to need counseling to get through the transition. You might think that, given their daytime performance, you wouldn't want small children in the same room in which you were trying to sleep. Not so! When they are sleeping, children are incredibly nice to be around. You can just admire them and glow with pride and love. And they can be very sweet when they wake up well rested, and before they remember that their life's work is to keep you on your toes. This five-second period is one of the highlights of my life.

The Irony of It All

One night the kids actually went to bed early. Wow! Freedom! What could we do with this precious time? We did what any other parent would do, we sat in the kitchen listening to the baby monitor hum. "Was that a cough? I thought I heard something. Do you think they're all right? I'm just going to go upstairs and check. I'll be right back. Then we'll ... we'll think of something to do."

Chapter Quiz: Sleep

You know, you could be sleeping now. Are you really sure you want to do this quiz? If you can stay awake all the way to the end, you pass. If you find yourself reading the same line over and over, you need to go to sleep. If you find yourself reading the same line over and over, you need to go to sleep. If you line yourself finding the same read over and over, you sleed to go to neep.

1. When you become a parent, the most important thing in your life becomes:
   a. Sex.
   b. Drugs (prescription, of course).
   c. Rock and roll.
   d. Sleep.

2. The best way to get some sleep is:
   a. Close your eyes, but not while operating a motor vehicle.
   b. Sleep when the baby sleeps and hire a large domestic staff to get things done.
   c. Go to work.
   d. Wait ten years.

Chapter 9

Food, Glorious Food

Cuisine de l'Enfant

Among its many other blessings, fatherhood gives you a chance to expand your culinary horizons. Without the excuse of having a child, who would dare be so adventurous as to try pureed peas on zwieback biscuit? Pureed squash on toast? Pureed carrot on shirt? Or, my favorite, pureed pear on a bed of today's newspaper?

Still, it's very satisfying to get to the solid food stage, round about six months. It gives you a real sense of providing sustenance to your child in a form that you can relate to—he's eating the same things you eat, only mooshed.

Feeding an infant makes you wonder about our concepts of eating versus species survival. What I mean is, you would think that eating would be a basic survival instinct, so the whole concept of "getting a child to eat" seems a bit silly. Like our species would become extinct if we didn't make airplane noises to get our young to open their mouths? Like that works, anyway.

So the way I see it, feeding time is not really about eating, so much as it is about establishing the concept of a meal, of a finite feeding time that has a beginning and an end. This compartmentalizing of our needs in many ways reflects our whole approach to the world, that you have to eat now, at this time, for the sake of convenience, so that we can all get on to other productive things. This isn't bad, mind you, it's part of the socialization process, the inherent conflict between the desires of the individual and the desires of the larger society. Left to our own devices, we would probably want to be able to eat whatever we wanted to eat whenever we wanted to eat it. Meals are a practical social phenomenon, but one that the baby's basic instincts tend to resist. This is why the entire jar of pureed sweet potato somehow seems to have missed its mark and has instead been instrumental in necessitating another entire load of laundry—your clothes, the baby's clothes, the tablecloth—and ... what's that on the ceiling?

The Mad Cow Diet

Let me tell you, my standards for a lot of things have gone down the drain since having children, and food is definitely one of those things. Before Kayla was born, I was a vegetarian. Not only was I a vegetarian, I soaked my beans overnight, then rinsed and cooked them for two hours before assembling the bean casserole which then had to be baked for an hour. Then somewhere along the line I realized that when dinner came along we were preparing four different meals. This was after Jacob was born. He ate baby food. Kayla ate kid food. My wife, having spent the last four years either being pregnant and/or breastfeeding and thereby requiring huge infusions of protein, had begun to eat meat again. And I was making beans and rice for me. And we wondered why we were so stressed at meal time.

Some day I may be a vegetarian again, but right now I am a convenience slut, so if a birthday party finds me at McDonald's Playland, saints preserve me, I'm going with the program. Oh, you don't know about birthday parties at McDonald's yet? Well, let me just say, they're everything you could imagine them to be, and more.

Whining and Dining

If you haven't had your first child yet, I suggest you immediately go out to a nice restaurant and have a fabulous, leisurely meal. Hand the waiter your camera to record this moment for posterity. Blow up the photo, frame it, and hang it in the dining room.

Because, believe me, after having kids you won't be able to so much as conjure up a vision of what it could possibly be like if you and your wife were actually able to sit down to dinner ... together ... alone ... in a restaurant ... and actually were able to eat the food that was in front of you.

On second thought, you might want to place the photo in the bathroom, because this is where you are likely to end up eating a lot of your meals. At least we do. Sometimes the only time the kids are stationary enough to be able to eat is when they're in the bathtub.

When we eat in a restaurant now we have learned to ask for take-out containers to be brought along with the food, since usually by the time the food has arrived one or more of the kids have fallen apart, as we say in parenting parlance, and we have to beat a hasty retreat before the evil parent appears. You will get to know the evil parent—it's the one that does all those things that you, the nice, enlightened, good parent wouldn't dream of doing. Like, *SCREAMING!!!*

Used Food

An important but surprisingly unheralded pleasure of fatherhood is that you become a repository for partially eaten foods. As a two-year-old, Jacob would take huge bites of something and then walk over to me (two-year-olds never eat sitting down, at least not mine) with mouth bulging and wait patiently for me to hold out my hand so that he could spit out the impossibly large wad of food, which I would gladly do because, let's face it, it's coming out, and better in my hand than on the rug where I will be the first person to step on it, probably barefoot. If anything could convince me to go out and get a dog, it would be so I could say, "Jake, just spit that wad of Tootsie Roll and oatmeal out on the floor—Rex will get it. REX!!! Come get some nummies! Good dog."

My wife's mother says that children "will eat the food right out of your mouth." Which would be fine. It's when they put food they've already chewed back into your mouth that I mind. Unless it contains chocolate.

And the backwash. Never surrender your glass of juice to a two-year-old who is eating unless you want a half-inch of sediment at the bottom of your glass. Oh, it's not a half-inch right away. It takes a while for the little brown particles to swirl gracefully down to the bottom.

Room Service

While my wife was in her breastfeeding stage, which lasted about five years, I found myself doing a lot of hunting and gathering in the kitchen to fuel the engines of milk production. It seemed that whenever she would settle in to nurse, suddenly she became ravenously hungry and needed for me to bring her something to eat. I always wondered if maybe the hunger really was there *before* she sat down, like while she could have gotten the food *herself,* but then perhaps that was just me being cynical and selfish and mean and irritable—I do get a teensy bit cranky now and again, when I haven't had my beauty sleep. Isn't that hard to believe?

It was during this time that we got an intercom. When I would hear a strange crackling noise and there were no cats in the room I would know it was my wife trying to summon me from upstairs. What she was saying was impossible to distinguish, but it was usually followed by my daughter yelling some message down the stairs at nine-thousand decibels, like, "Bring up some food! Mommy wants some food! Cheese and an apple!"

Service with a smile, that's me ... on a good day, anyway.

Chapter Quiz: Food

If you can complete this quiz without spilling any food on it, you pass.

1. When you become a parent, the *least* important thing in your life becomes:
   a. Sex.
   b. Drugs.
   c. Rock and roll.
   d. Food.
   e. All of the above.

2. The best way to get a good meal when you have small children is:
   a. Take the kids to Le Chateau and order the Macaroni avec Fromage.
   b. Eat when the baby sleeps and hire a large domestic staff to get things done.
   c. Go to work.
   d. Wait ten years.

Chapter 10

Sex (Really!)

The Prurient Parent

Aha! You turned to this chapter first, didn't you? Well if you're interested in sex and you're in a bookstore trying to decide whether or not to buy this book, BUY IT! It's FULL of juicy sex! If there's one thing that can be said about this book, it's that it is full of it!

The good news is, there is still sex after childbirth. The bad news is that you are not the ones having it. Ha ha! Just kidding!

Occasionally you will have the energy to cuddle up to your spouse in bed. These interludes used to go something like this:

"Mmmm," she murmurs.
"Mmmm," he responds.
"Ooooh!"
"Oooooh!"
"Aaaaaaaah!"
"Aaaaaaaaaah!"
"Wheee whoopeeee zooooooooom!!!"

Now they go something like this.
"Mmmm," she murmurs.
"Mmmm," he responds.
"Zzzzz..."
"Zzzzzzzzzzz..."

If you don't understand what I'm saying, turn to the chapter on Sleep.

But come Saturday night, you may get lucky. Or that special Sunday afternoon when both kids are napping at the same time, and there is a harmonic convergence of the planets!

Interrup-*Waaaaa!*-tions

Of course, there always looms the danger of the interruption. My theory is that it is essentially in a child's best interest, survival-wise, to have as few siblings to compete with as possible. Therefore, the child, even at the infant stage, has the instinct to prevent further procreational activities by its parents. That's the bad news.

The good news, if you can call it that, is that interruptions are such a part of the father's life that he kind of gets used to it. So, that being the case and since I always liked science, I have taken the trouble to classify some of the more common interruptions:

Common Parental Interruptions	
Dinus interruptus	Unfinished meal
Conversus interruptus	Unfinished conversation
Coitus interruptus	Doesn't happen as often as you might think, mostly due to the next condition:
Coitus non-startus	You get the picture

For more on sex when you have children, see the chapter on Sleep.

Chapter Quiz: Sex

For a more intimate test-taking experience, take this quiz with your spouse—but only if she's already awake!

1. The purpose of sex is to:
   a. Procreate.
   b. Recreate.
   c. Redecorate.
   d. Sell merchandise.

2. You and your spouse will have the opportunity to have sex:
   a. When the children are asleep.
   b. When the children are at someone else's house.
   c. When the children are asleep at someone else's house.
   d. When hell freezes over, if you can stay awake.

Chapter 11

Family Finances

The Hidden Costs of Parenthood

It's expensive having kids. It's not so much the things you would expect, like clothes and all that. Most of the clothes you get as presents, then take to the Salvation Army where you can pick out something more tasteful.

It's the hidden costs that get you, such as guilt tipping. Guilt tipping refers to the fact that when you eat out, you have to tip waitpersons about 120 percent due to the mess you're leaving. Waitpersons take note: Get us fed and out of the restaurant before one of the children explodes and you will be able to send your child to an Ivy League school.

Another hidden cost is temporary parental insanity. I am sure that every parent experiences this—those moments when, in a fog of sentimentality and material lust, and maybe a little ego, you buy the big thing. You know what I mean—the BIG thing. The $250 doll house that will make your little girl's eyes light up. The $500 little motorized Mercedes convertible? Or the $1800 swing set, which is a lot like the $1500 one but it has that extra thing on it, that thing the children will just love playing on and remember all their lives, and they'll have you to thank, what a great dad you'll be if you buy it, and having seen the $1800 and $1500 ones, how could you even consider the $269 one? What sort of a father would history remember you as having been?

Whoa! Snap out of it! Unless you can pay cash, that is.

Investments Tips

Here's a major money-making tip, free with the purchase of this book: Buy stock in Baby Gap now. I would myself, but it would probably violate insider trading laws, since I know so many women who are pregnant.

Also on the buy list: Disney, Mattel. All of your money goes to them anyway, one way or another. You may as well own a piece of the action.

Mattel may make toys other than Barbie, but I doubt that they need to. I was astonished to learn that little girls do not have a single Barbie for whom they then buy inexpensive little outfits. They have multiple Barbies, multiple dozens of Barbies—Bubble Magic Barbie, Veterinarian Barbie, Rock Star Barbie, and so on. Or you can get the "So Much To Do" Barbie playset, which basically consists of a living room with a TV in it.

Do I approve of Barbie? Can I approve of any doll whose male counterpart is considered an accessory (Ken's box identifies him as a "Barbie Ken"—and how come he has this plastic hair, like he's not even a companion, just some kind of a mannequin for Barbie to be seen with)? Not to mention what it does to little girls' self-image when they think they have to grow up to look like Barbie, whose real-life-sized measurements would be impossible to match even if you were a cross between Dolly Parton and an anorexic fashion model.

But I figure that the allure of Barbie is that to a four-year-old she represents a grown-up who can be manipulated and controlled, and who doesn't talk back. Fairly compelling, you must admit.

So if you're a socially conscious investor, you can make up your own mind about Barbie. Hey, at least she doesn't smoke. Well, except for Cigar Shop Barbie.

As for Disney, every movie they've made recently has scared the bejeezus out of my kids, but I certainly wouldn't bet against their stock, on the grounds that they control half of the known universe. The other half, of course, belongs to Microsoft. When the two merge, it's time to beam up.

Money = Power

We have found the secret to successful shopping with children, which is, give your kids money! Really! Start them on an allowance at age 4 and let them decide what to spend it on. Then they don't bug you for every little thing when you're in a store. This really works! We give them a dollar for each year of their age which may sound like a lot at first, but the catch is they have to put 1/4th away for college, 1/4th for charity, and 1/4th for medium-term savings, leaving 1/4th to spend in a lustful consumer fashion. So while Kayla, at age 6, was bummed out to learn that she couldn't buy Life-Size Barbie for $2.00, she was able to shift her focus to "what can I buy with this $2.00" rather than being hung up on "I want something and the only way to get it is to whine my parents into submission." Besides, she probably figured that Grandma would be an easier touch.

This empowers the child, and is a heck of a lot cheaper in the long run, because it is a well-known fact that whining can produce temporary insanity in adults, resulting in unpredictable behavior patterns ranging from rather embarrassing public acting out to irrational purchasing decisions. Another plus is, we don't have to build an addition onto the house for Life-Size Barbie.

Teaching Kids about Investing

There actually is a popular children's song that pretty well sums up investing in the stock market:
The itsy bitsy spider climbed up the water spout
Bull market
Down came the rain and washed the spider out
Bear market

Out came the sun and dried up all the rain
Low inflation, strong earnings
And the itsy bitsy spider climbed up the spout again.
Moral: stay invested for the long term.

The Upside

Having children actually can free you from certain money worries, like balancing your checkbook. I didn't balance mine for at least a year after our first child. What a relief!

Chapter Quiz: Money

Test your money knowledge. For every correct answer, please send the author $10 in check or money order.

1. The purpose of money is to:
    a. Buy toys.

2. The stock market is a good investment because:
    a. Over time it provides the best return.
    b. Everyone else does it.
    c. My hairstylist passes me inside information.
    d. OTB is closed at this hour.

3. A good financial motto to remember is:
    a. Buy low, sell high.
    b. The check is in the mail.
    c. I can't be overdrawn, I still have checks left!
    d. The wheels on the bus go round and round.

Chapter 12

Power, Love, Truth, and All That

Sure You're Tense, Irritable...

Remember the old aspirin commercial? "Sure you're tense, irritable, but don't take it out on the children!" Take drugs instead! This was a brilliant marketing ploy, to use the guilt that all parents feel when they yell at their children and use it to sell little white pills.

It can be difficult not to be consumed by your own anger and frustration when a child is screaming and being totally irrational at 3 a.m. She wakes up because she's hungry, because you failed to get her to eat a proper dinner, and she won't eat now, either. You offer yogurt. "No! Cereal!" You prepare cereal. She won't eat it. "Do a puzzle!" But will she do the puzzle while sitting at her little table, like usual? No, it has to be done while sitting on your lap on the couch, but of course she can't reach it. "Move it closer!" And then, "No, not THAT puzzle!"

Remember, now, I am fortyish and have not had a full night's sleep in about two years. This is why they give you little brochures at the hospital telling you: "Don't shake the baby." I swear they really do. I couldn't understand it myself at first.

My own personal and totally original theory—which I may have stolen from somewhere, I don't remember—is that the inherent conflict you feel as a parent is genetically based. You have two sets of genes, or at least two tendencies encoded in your genes. One set is designed to ensure *your* survival as an organism. The other is designed to ensure the survival of the *species*. The former, designed for your survival, is what gives you the urge to discipline your child in a way that would make the police blotter; this is sometimes known as "going postal." The latter, species survival, is what prevents you. There is constant dynamic tension between these two forces. You, the current carrier of your piece of the gene pool, are caught in the middle of this millennia-old conflict. Fortunately, there is medication for it.

(I also have a theory that the earth is a giant compost pile and humans are basically the worms, but I think that one deserves a book of its own.)

Basic Parenting Philosophy

So this is where discipline comes in. But you know all about that—we're all walking encyclopedias on that subject. Besides, standing in the corner is passé. That went out with calling children "bad." Now we do time outs. While on the surface a time out and a stand in the corner may seem like the same thing—the child must go someplace and remain quiet and still for a certain length of time—there is a major difference.

A time out is basically a stand in the corner that has been to some self-help seminars. It is a time of introspection and self-change, rather than of punishment and humiliation when something external is forcing you to change. In the time out, you are regrouping, talking to your inner coach, before continuing the game. Standing in the corner is like being benched for being a poor sport.

So which is better—the old way or the new? Need you even ask? We, of course, must do things totally differently from the way our parents did them to ensure that our kids will turn out just like us! Got that?

An Innovative Child Management Technique

I have developed a highly effective parenting technique which occasionally affords me a period of undisturbed adult functioning long enough to at least prevent total domestic and financial collapse. I call this technique "candying."

Candying is a powerful technique that cannot be used all the time, and so must be reserved for times when you absolutely have to get something done without interruption. You get a large bag of candy, place it on the floor where the children can reach it, and then, whatever you do, *don't look!* Just go about your task. When you are finished with your task, you remove the bag. Easy? You bet! Remember not to look, though, or your good-parent reflexes might ruin the whole plan. Also, make sure the dog is not in the house at the time.

Tips on Child Raising

To raise a child, hold it firmly under the armpits and lift, being careful to bend at the knees rather than straining your back. There, that's my advice on raising a child. You can also adapt this to moving furniture, which probably makes it the most useful child-raising advice you'll ever get. (Don't even ask about child-*rearing*.)

For the most part, your children are going to learn by your example, but they get to choose which examples. Therefore, I suggest you remember the following points:

Never say anything you don't want to hear your children say, even if they're out of earshot.

Never say anything you don't want to hear your children say in front of, or to, their grandparents.

Never say anything you don't want to hear shouted in unison by your children and their friends at 4000 decibels.

Let's face it, you can make kids conform to any behavior you want, but—get ready for some bad news here—they aren't likely to turn out to be any more emotionally healthy than you are, so get your own act together first.

Me, I gave up drinking and smoking, not to mention sloth, envy, pride, gluttony, covetousness, lust, and anger. Not only has this made me a happier, healthier person and a better role model, but also my wife has not thrown me out. Besides, who has time for vice?

Teaching Values

Good values are important, so I always look in the 3-for-$5 bin at the toy store at the mall.

Boys Will Be Boys

I think it's a special challenge for us fathers to teach our sons to channel their natural aggression in healthy ways. I will leave it to you to determine whether or not aspiring to become a professional hockey player is healthy.

I have a boy and a girl, and let me tell you, boys need to hit things. With Jacob, it's usually me. And his little fists are right about at groin level, if you catch my drift. If he's mad about something, like he can't get Batman's cape on, you had better not say a word or he will go quite a distance out of his way to come over and pummel you soundly.

I try to encourage him to vent his frustration on the pillows, but that suggestion just further infuriates him, especially if he hasn't had a nap.

When I was a kid I spent most of my time playing with toy soldiers and tanks, or playing army, during which the most fun part was getting killed and dying dramatically. My brother and I both had "gun drawers" full of plastic hand grenades, pistols, bullet holders, you name it. We had BB-guns, bows and arrows, knives and swords of every description, and countless armies—from the Civil War, WW I, WW II (the Brits, the Americans, the

Germans, even the Afrika Korps), complete with scale model aircraft, tanks, howitzers, battleships, the whole scene. The sets came with soldiers engaged in every imaginable warlike activity, and there were even dead ones. You would think I would have turned out to be Ghengis Rambo or something, but as I had a gentle and essentially nonviolent father, I ended up being pretty peace-loving. It would seem that the values you teach your children and the way you yourself treat other living beings will have a lot more effect on your child's tendency toward violence than their toys.

My conclusion is that it's okay for my peace-loving kid to own a small arsenal but your kid, with *his* emotional problems and hostility, had better stick to Mr. Potato Head.

Telling the Truth

Enlightened parent that I am, I make it a point always to be up-front with my children. No phony bribes or threats. No white lies. Besides, they're smarter than I am and they can see through all that.

I do, however, rely heavily on spelling of words that are, for one reason or another, hot buttons. As in, "Should we take Kayla for I-C-E C-R-E-A-M or is it too close to bedtime?" This particular dodge doesn't work anymore, however, because now anytime we spell anything, she assumes we're talking about ice cream. For example, I'll say, "Shall we give this S-T-U-P-I-D outfit from Aunt Millie to Goodwill?" and Kayla will yell, "Yeah! Ice cream! Let's go for ice cream!"

Also, it's important to remember that spelling doesn't work on adults. Once I wanted to ask my wife if she had gotten a certain present for a friend who was in the room at the time. "Did you get the P-U-Z-Z-L-E for Jenny?" I asked. "I can spell," Jenny reminded me. Jenny is 26 years old and was an honor student at Cornell. It's great to know that they still teach spelling in college, at least in the Ivy League.

CHAPTER 13

Mothers-in-Law

Ha! You probably think I'm about to bad-mouth mothers-in-law! What, do you think I'm crazy? I have one, and she can read, and despite my best efforts she will probably find out that I wrote this book. So I'm here to tell you that mothers-in-law are wonderful, loving, helpful, and generous. Once properly trained, they're great to have around.

From what *other* people say (I personally wouldn't know), I believe a great need exists for mother-in-law training. Perhaps a Mother-in-Law University (why not—McDonald's has a Hamburger University, and mothers-in-laws are much more teachable than hamburger). Course titles could include "Letting Your Daughter Do It Herself," "Letting Your Daughter-in-Law Do It Herself," "Helping Out without Attaching Strings," and of course, "Sending Money: How Much Is Enough?"

Fortunately, my mother-in-law does not need this training, right Grandma? Funny chapter, right Grandma? Ha, ha.

I think I'll just stop *riiiiight* here.

Chapter 14

FAQs–Frequently Asked Questions about Fatherhood

Will I still be able to play cards with the boys every Friday night?
Sure, sure, as long as it's okay with your wife. Why don't you go ask her? I'll wait right here.

Can you recommend a good orthodontist? I seem to be missing some teeth.
Sorry about that.

Will I have to change diapers?
Not if you keep them clean.

No, I mean on the baby.
Why don't you go and ask your wife.

Well, uh, never mind.
It's not that bad.

Will I be able to watch sports on TV?
Yes, but your eyes will be closed.

Will I still be able to have stop and have a beer now and then?
Now, yes. Then, no.

Why do new fathers wear eye black underneath their eyes—do they play a lot of football?
That's not eye black, that's bags. You're not getting this, are you?

Will my wife and I still have time to talk about books, the arts, politics, philosophy?

The good news is, you still will have some time for meaningful adult discourse. The bad news is, by that time, the bright light of your intellect will not have enough wattage to power a night light. Also, you and your wife will be constitutionally incapable of having any conversation that is not about your children for the next twenty years.

Should I be scared about fatherhood?

Only if you take me too seriously, which I don't advise. Fatherhood is probably the greatest thing you will ever experience. You'll find that everything I said in this book is true, but it won't matter. You will totally love it. It's hard to explain.